T0065269

God's
Bow and Arrow

Randy Brown

GOD'S BOW AND ARROW

iUniverse books may be ordered through booksellers or by contacting:

iUniverse
1663 Liberty Drive
Bloomington, IN 47403
www.iuniverse.com
844-349-9409

Scripture quotations marked KJV are from the Holy Bible, King James Version (Authorized Version). First published in 1611. Quoted from the KJV Classic Reference Bible, Copyright © 1983 by The Zondervan Corporation.

ISBN: 978-1-6632-2836-9 (sc)
ISBN: 978-1-6632-2837-6 (e)

Print information available on the last page.

iUniverse rev. date: 09/16/2021

My prayer is that as you read this booklet you will ask the Holy Spirit to move upon you and speak to you, and that you will find the knowledge of God overflowing in you so that you might catch the revelation and be filled with wisdom, that God might unlock to you that which seems a mystery, that it might become enlightenment to you. Hallelujah!

Contents

The Bible says, "This is the day which the Lord hath made; we will rejoice and be glad in it" (Ps. 118:24).

I thank God for his goodness, for He is truly a good God. During this present hour I seem to be in a season of prophecy whereby God desires me to actually put the prophetic utterances in paperback form. When this word I'm about to share with you came forth, immediately I was going to share it with our church family. But the Lord said to me, "Randy, this is to be done like the first; put this in paperback form also." So I'm asking that as you read this material the anointing of the Holy Spirit will awaken your spirit-man to something that is happening right now. We are entering into it more so than ever before right here in our Long Island area as well as in other parts of the United States. I pray that the Holy Spirit will provoke you to good works through this prophetic word that God is having me speak.

God's Bow
and Arrow

P salms 7:10-12 says, "My defense is of God, which saveth the upright in heart. God judgeth the righteous, and God is angry with the wicked every day. If he turn not, he will whet his sword; he hath bent his bow, and made it ready."

As we were about to enter the year 1991, the Lord gave me a vision and prophetic word: He showed me the bow of God bent back and allowed me to watch as it released an arrow. Psalms 7:13 says, "He hath also prepared for him the instruments of death; he ordaineth his arrows against the persecutors." This verse from Psalms 7 indicates that God's bow is ready and that He is going to send His arrows out against the persecutors and troublemakers. The rest of the vision that came before me and the word that came from the vision is as follows: I saw launched from a huge bow in heaven an arrow of great size. This arrow came down at supernatural speed streaking through the atmosphere toward planet earth. It struck with great force in the center of Long Island. I then actually saw one thing happen and heard a second thing.

The first thing, which I saw, was blood gushing forth from the Long Island area. The second thing, which I heard, was the cries and screams of people coming up from the Island, crying out, "Help us, we are perishing. Help us, we are dying."

The Lord began to speak to me saying, "Randy, My son, My day of return is nigh and judgment will come. Though many don't believe, My hand of judgment shall be manifested and revealed on the earth as well as before the throne of heaven in due time." He then said, "Before people perish, Randy, and before people die without knowing their Savior, I'm about to release one of the greatest evangelistic moves Long Island has ever seen." The Lord told me that the bow and arrow meant that His judgment is on the way, that He is going to judge people for their sins. But His word promised that all shall hear the gospel *before* His second coming. That's why I believe there must be a great bursting forth of evangelism.

3

I'm not just talking about tents and crusades. I'm talking about one-on-one witnessing-people taking the gospel to people; believers walking the streets inviting unbelievers to come to the house of the Lord. I see witnessing coming forth from the Body universal unlike ever before. If we can get our selves ready for what God is about to do, awesome things are going to happen. If you have never believed that you could be used of God, you're about to see something that's going to blow your mind. God is going to be using everyone who will yield himself to Him as a vessel to win somebody to Jesus. This must happen before the cries and screams go out and no one can be helped. God is going to be using people like you to win people to Jesus. *Hallelujah!*

I now want to fill you with Scriptures. I want you to read these important verses. Memorize them if you can. Allow them to bear witness in your spirit. I want you to look at the Word, hear what God has to say, and grab hold of it in Jesus' name.

For I am not ashamed of the gospel of Christ: for it is the power of God unto salvation to everyone that believeth; to the Jew first, and also to the Greek.

Romans 1:16

For there is no respect of persons with God.

Romans 2:11

As it is written, There is none righteous, no, not one: There is none that understandeth, there is none that seeketh after God. They are all gone out of the way, they are together become unprofitable; there is none that doeth good, no, not one.

Romans 3:10-12

There is the power within God's word to the pulling down of strongholds, to the casting down of imaginations, and to the keeping of darkness under your feet. God will free people from sin if we give them His word, and they come to Jesus. If we give them God's word, they *will* come to Jesus. I see this unlike the way I've seen it before.

Saying, Blessed are they whose iniquities are forgiven, and whose sins are covered. Blessed is the man to whom the Lord will not impute sin.

Romans 4:7-8

For when we were yet without strength, in due time Christ died for the ungodly.

Romans 5:6

But God commendeth His love toward us, in that, while we were yet sinners, Christ died for us. Much more then, being now justified by His blood, we shall be saved from wrath through Him. For if, when we were enemies, we were reconciled to God by the death of His Son, much more, being reconciled, we shall be saved by His life. A.nd not only so, but we also joy in God through our Lord Jesus Christ, by Whom we have now received the atonement.

Romans 5:8-11

God has launched His arrow. I saw it as clearly as you see this page. I saw an arrow of judgment launched from heaven, yet Romans 5:9 says, "Much more then, being now justified by His blood, we shall be saved from wrath through Him." If anyone has told you that God does not get angry, then that person has not read the Bible. The Lord our God wants to give us the victory over everything the enemy is using to hold us down. All we have to do is open up our spirits and receive the revelation of truth and knowledge. Romans 5:10 says, For if, when we were enemies, we were reconciled to God by the death of His Son, much more, being reconciled, we shall be saved by His life." (Also see the following verses from the Book of Romans:

6:23; 7:4; 8:6,9; 9:25, 27; 10:9; 11:11; 12:21; 13:11,14; 14:7; and 15:7.)

I believe that God wants to use you as His local evangelist to your family, your neighborhood, and your entire town. I hope you're hearing what I'm saying. I hope these words are gripping your heart as they have gripped mine. Acts 1:18 says that we should be witnesses in Jerusalem-that's your immediate family; to Judea-that's your neighborhood; and to Samaria-that's further out, going outside your neighborhood into your town, your county, even out of the boundaries of your state.

God wants you to be His evangelist right now! And all you have to do is be obedient and hear what *Thus saith the Lord.*

You may wish to pray before reading this next section. In fact, it would be good for you to pray and worship a little while before you read it so that the same anointing of the Father which quickened me to speak might be upon you that you could discern how it fits into your life.

"For thus saith the Lord your God, even the God of Abraham, the God that has made covenants and promises throughout generations after generations, saith the Lord. Have not I spoken My word to you, and you say, 'Lord when have you spoken your word to me?' For My word is for My Bride. And if you are My Bride, then I have spoken My word to you. My Bride, there are others that are to be a part of you, that are still out in the world, that are lost, saith the Lord. And even I the Lord your God am about to launch an arrow. Even I your Lord and your God am about to launch an arrow. I shall even launch an arrow from heaven, saith the Lord. And it shall strike your area. Someone needs to hear the word of salvation, saith the Lord your God. Who will go for Me and whom can I send? saith the Lord. Who will go for Me and whom will I send? saith the Lord your God. Will you hearken to My voice today? Will you take up the blood stained banner and carry it? saith the Lord. Will you take up your cross and carry it as even I the Lord would ask you to do so? How long will you sit to the side and say, 'Lord, I'm not ready. I'm not worthy. There are others that are greater and more powerful than me.' But I the Lord your God send you to your family. I send others to their neighborhoods. I send some to stand on street corners. I send some to hand out tracts. I send some to leave home and travel abroad. Not even just abroad as far as over the water, saith the Lord. But abroad as to different parts of the U.S. My people are perishing; they're dying. And the time has come near that even I the Lord your God would allow the trump to be blown that My Son might be sent back to take My Bride unto Himself. Bride, are you ready? And I know you *are,* says the Lord. Even get others ready. As you are ready and you wear a garment without spot and blemish, saith the Lord, even so get others ready, that they may also receive salvation and be not left behind, but find themselves caught up with you also to be gathered together to meet the Lord their God in the air, saith the Lord. For even I the Lord your God, even I Jesus, come quickly saith the Lord.

I pray that this writing is a blessing to you that it opens your mind, your spirit and your understanding. I pray that the anointing of the Father would rest upon you now and draw you closer unto Himself. May He bless you and keep you.

The Four Waves

The day that I am writing this is September 1, 1990. It is the 18th day of a fast that God put me on. I have partaken of nothing but water and juice. As you receive this prophetic utterance, let it be enlightenment to you that you might receive the knowledge and the blessings of the Father, in Jesus' name.

I'm going to read out of First Peter 4:10-11:

As every man hath received the gift, even so minister the same one to another, as good stewards of the manifold grace of God. If any man speak, let him speak as the oracles of God; if any man minister, let him do it as of the ability which God giveth: that God in all things may be glorified through Jesus Christ, to Whom be praise and dominion for ever and ever. Amen.

I Peter 4:10-11

As the shepherd of the flock at Bread of Life Fellowship, I am going to minister this word in the manifold grace of God-in the multiples of His keeping grace and power. I am going to speak in the fashion of prophetic oracles. I am going to minister according to the ability that God has given me. In all that you are about to receive, receive it as from the Father. I believe that it will bear witness heavily with your spirit as you read. In all that I'm about to say, Jesus Christ will be glorified. I believe that the oracles that follow deal mainly with the Long Island area and the ministries of the people in that area. I believe they pertain primarily to the work of God right before you go into Queens, to the end of Suffolk County before you hit the water. I really believe that.

The Lord would have me to say that there are four powerful waves about to come crashing over the Long Island area. They will bring with them some unholiness, but there will be some holiness in them too. The Lord has shown me these four tremendous, powerful, massive waves coming over the Island in the near future. I believe that these prophecies will be fulfilled between the years of 1991and 1995. I'm not saying the four waves will come in this order, but I believe they will all come during the first half of the 90's.

The First Wave

The first wave is *racism*. I believe that an ugly yet powerful wave of it is coming. What I'm talking about is prejudice: against whites, blacks, Orientals, Hispanics, you name it. A terrible demonic force of prejudice, bigotry and racism has already moved into the New York State area, but Long Island has been shielded from a lot of it. It has been mostly in the city areas, but I see a crash of forceful waves coming our way. And it won't only strike the world and their schools, communities, and institutions. I see the church-world going through a violent outbreak of bigotry. I have confidence, how ever, that God is going to be raising up some powerful, anointed works that will be beautifully blended bodies of believers of many races under one roof. This is the only thing that is going to keep Long Island from being tom apart. I see the Spirit of God as a tremendous moving force, and I believe the churches need to be aware of it. If they are not, many may find themselves falling or being deceived. This spirit of racism will affect many in the church-world. I believe you will see the "true colors" of some so-called born-again, Spirit-filled believers in Christ Jesus.

I believe we need to pray. I'm in a series of prayer meetings with my congregation right now and if we have ever prayed, the time to do it is now! We need to pray that God would keep our church bodies from this divisive spirit and cause us to move in His Spirit. This move of the enemy is coming soon, and we need to hold our shields of faith high, hold fast the sword of the Spirit, keep our minds covered with the helmet of salvation, get the breastplate of righteousness on, gird our loins with truth, and shod our *feet,* which represents our walk with God, with the preparation of the gospel of peace. This is what will destroy y the enemy as he comes in. That is the first wave of the flood that is coming to our area between the years 1991and 1995.

The Second Wave

The second wave that I see coming is a heavy division between the churches on the Island. It won't be just because of bigotry and racism, but I see a division, a separating, a splitting. Churches will cease to fellowship with one another and will actually begin speaking against their brothers. Instead of preaching Jesus, I see an unsettling wave. I'm not talking about those who are blatantly ungodly. If I know of an ungodly work in the area, I will not hesitate to mention it to my people even if that might be offensive to some.

What I see, however, is an actual division where true men of God actually chew each other up in their pulpits because of slight differences of doctrinal belief.

I believe this wave is already on Long Island. I see a definite separating amongst the churches of God's people. There are those who are trying to force their hand. They say, "If I cannot be the leader of this entire Island, then I will not be on the Island at all. If I can't run the show; if everyone's attention can't be on me, then no one will have any attention on them." That attitude is unholy and ungodly. I already see it moving across the people of God on the Island, and it's mainly coming from two areas: pastors who are not living a pure life and are therefore allowing the devil to cause a spirit of division to come into them; and pastors who are allowing their congregations to entertain spirits of division and schisms. Also, these pastors must be not only confronted from the platform, but they must be confronted personally that all may know who is causing contention in the household of faith.

Those who are in the ministry of intercession, those who are prayer warriors in the house of God, who have been specially anointed to pray, must be about their ministry. I believe that through prayer, this wave can actually be stifled in many churches. I want you to hear these words and grasp them because the Holy Spirit doesn't want His people caught off guard. The Bible says that God's own people perish for lack of knowledge. I hate to see God's people perishing because they have no knowledge of the works of the enemy, and because they will not hearken to the voice of the Most High. Let us hear and respond!

The Third Wave

The third wave that I see coming down with mighty impact on the Island is going to be the closing of works-the works of God. I see an economic crash coming down on the Island whereby people find themselves in such financial difficulty that many small churches will suffer greatly. When I say small churches, I'm talking of those with congregations under five hundred. These churches are going to find themselves in such financial struggles that the only thing that's going to help them is the wisdom and knowledge of those who are well-acquainted with the things of God. I'm speaking of those who understand what God's word says about being stewards, not robbing God of His tithes and offerings, making sacrificial *gifts,* being like the little women who gave her last mite. She didn't give of her abundance, but of her poverty. That's why He called her blessed. It's like the women who made the little cake of the last of her meal and oil for her and her son to eat. Then they were going to die. But a prophet came along and said, "Make the cake for me." The woman made the cake for him, and she prospered during the economic drought that was upon the land of Israel.

I see a similar drought coming, and I believe we must prepare ourselves spiritually. We might bend, but in the name of Jesus Christ we cannot be broken. All of this is to give glory to His name.

I see works closing because of the effect this drought will have on the people. There will be works that will literally close their doors. People will fall from the faith because of the struggle to survive financially during this drought. Be prepared children of God. Be ready. Let us not allow the enemy to be so subtle that he lulls us to sleep and causes us to miss the delivering power of God that will bring us through in time of need.

The Fourth Wave

These words are capable of filtering out to many other areas. We are going to see portions of all four of these waves around the United States. Maybe it's because I'm a Long Island pastor that I feel that God is speaking to me for this particular area. But I believe that we will see things fulfilled out of these writings-that one day your reading this will actually cause you to say, "'This was said through the lips of God's servant, and now we're seeing it on the news and hearing it on the streets." I see all four waves crashing violently onto the Long Island area.

I see a new move in leadership, mainly in the area of apostles and prophets. Don't misunderstand me, there is always going to be a five-fold ministry. There will always be apostles, prophets, evangelists, pastors and teachers. But I see a raising up of new apostles and new prophets in the Kingdom of God. Here on Long Island there have been apostles and prophets, but (and they can say what they want) God says, "You have failed Me, for even the Lord your God would say that you have failed Me. What have I told you to do and what have I told you not to do? How have I told you to move and how did I tell you not to move? And so in not being obedient to My voice, you, yes even you My apostle and you My prophet, you have failed even the Lord your God. And even that which has been handed to you on a golden platter in the presence of your Father; even handed to you to carry not only to the areas around you but even know that the Lord your God will take it, remove it and hand it to another. For because of your lack luster efforts and your carnal ways and your failures to stay in My presence, even I will judge you. Not only will you be judged in the world to come, saith the Lord your God, but you shall be judged now and that which has been given to you shall be removed and given unto another that is willing to use it, saith the Lord.

I see a raising up of new apostles and prophets here in the Long Island area and across the entire United States. Here on Long Island I see seven prophetesses that God is going to raise up, though they are unknown to us right now. At this point people don't even look on them as if they could be prophetesses, but I see seven prophetesses being raised up in this area. At least three or four of them will become internationally known. Three will make a dynamic impact on the local church body and will cause the Island to be shaken by the power of God. God says that He is raising up apostles and prophets afresh for this day and hour.

This is the fourth wave coming to the Long Island area. Some of these waves will strike other portions of the U.S., but God will always be our Lord and our Savior. As long as Jesus is King of kings and Lord of lords, that which needs to be will come to pass at the proper time. Brethren, let's stay strong before God. Let's keep our minds on Him, and see what He is doing. Let's be watchful.

I gave out a pamphlet once before about prophetic utterance. People called and wrote me saying, "Vie can see it; we've seen this happening: My brothers and sisters in Christ, let us be wise as serpents yet gentle as the Holy Ghost, that God would continue to bless us and keep us. Until we speak again or until I see you in the future, I pray that the grace of our Lord and Savior Jesus Christ and the sweet presence of the Holy Spirit abide over you from this day forth and for ever and ever in Jesus' most holy and precious name. Amen and amen.

The Forerunner

To God be the glory and all the praises unto His most holy and precious name. I want you to be blessed as you read this booklet; I want it to be encouragement and strength to you; and I want the hand of God to give revelation to you. I believe that God's Spirit is doing some wonderful things in these days, and as we are faithful to what the Spirit of the Lord is doing, we shall indeed be blessed.

Today's date as I begin this writing is February 26, 1991. I believe the Holy Spirit is going to do great and mighty things. As you read the pages that follow, allow the Holy Spirit to lead you into new revelations and blessings-all in line with God's holy Word. Receive and be blessed in Jesus name. Amen.

What I'm about to share with you is what the Spirit of the Lord quickened unto me. The Spirit of the Lord said to me, "'The forerunner." And immediately again the Holy Spirit of God said, "The forerunner." Late one evening as I was in my home resting and relaxing and having a peaceful night, the Holy Spirit said, "Randy, be the forerunner: He then began to move upon me concerning four areas, which God says we need to be attentive of. Some are happening already, but are going to really explode in a manner we can hardly believe during in the next several months to the next few years. When I say the next several years, I mean possibly the late 1990's. actually see these things when I speak these words and look over these prophetic utterances God has quickened in me. I see ahead to 1997 and a tremendous shaking of God in these areas.

The First Utterance

The first thing that God said to me was, "The forerunner. The Holy Spirit then directed me to Isaiah 40:

The voice of him that crieth in the wilderness, Prepare ye the way of the Lord, make straight in the desert a highway for our God. Every valley shall be exalted, and every mountain and hill shall be made low: and the crooked shall be made straight, and the rough places plain.

Isaiah 40:3-4

These verses are first of all telling us that Jesus is coming. Even as John was the forerunner of the first coming, we are the forerunners of the second coming. Not me myself, but we as the Church are the forerunners of the second coming of Jesus Christ. Verse four says that the valleys will be exalted. Everyone who thinks they're not doing any thing, every person who believes he's been given just a small work to do, God says He is going to exalt you. If you keep yourself humble, in due time you will be exalted. Those things that seem like they are nothing are very much something to God. He is about to exalt the works that natural man looks away from. He is about to abase the works that natural man tries to lift up. Nothing can be truly lifted up unless God Himself does the lifting. The works that we think are going to shake the area, God says He is going to bring down. The works that we think God is not going to use and won't amount to anything, God is going to raise up. Isaiah 40 continues:

And the glory of the Lord shall be revealed, and all flesh shall see it together: for the mouth of the Lord hath spoken it. The voice said, Cry. And he said, What shall I cry? All flesh is grass, and all the goodliness thereof is as the flower of the field. The grass withereth, the flower fadeth: because the Spirit of the Lord bloweth upon it: surely the people is grass.

Isaiah 40:5-7

God is sending out people to be forerunners of the second coming. This is the first utterance that the Spirit of the Lord is saying. Be attentive and listen to what the Spirit of the Lord is saying.

The Second Utterance

This second utterance comes from Second Timothy 4. All of the areas God gave me to share are powerful and important, but I believe that this second one, if it is not done, will cause the other three parts to fall to the way side null and void. Second Timothy 4:7 says, "I have fought a good fight, I have finished my course, I have kept the faith."

I have finished my course; that is the word for part two of your reading. I heard the Lord say, "They won't finish what I gave them to do. They claim to be tired. They claim to be weary. They claim it's too difficult, that I've given them too much to do and not enough help. But I know that these are lying spirits. God wants His people to finish what He has given them to do. He wants us to stop doing half the job and start finishing it.

That's the second utterance and it's very simple by itself: Stop doing half the job and start finishing the job. Many of us can relate to that, for we have been given jobs to do for the Lord, but half way through have lost interest. Or maybe we thought there were too many road blocks in the way. Second Timothy 4:7 starts off, "I have fought a good fight. You'll never finish your course unless you fight a good fight. So let us finish what God has given us to do. I keep a book in which I record all the prophecies God has given me over the years. I confess that there are still things that I have to do, and the only legitimate thing that can stop them from being done is if I die or if Jesus comes. These things must get done. Let us finish our course, so that we can be faithful servants, honorable vessels unto God. "For yeah, even the Spirit of the Lord would say in these times and in these last days, I look for a man, even I the Lord God look for a woman; I look for a vessel of honor, saith the Lord, one that will speak the word by the word; one that will speak the word with the word; and one that will make the word be only what is spoken-word upon word upon word, saith the Lord. For I am indeed tired, saith God, of them that have played with My word and cut up My word and tried to circumcise and reshape and reform and remold My word, saith the Lord. But I send out, even I send out as swords of fire, saith *God,* men and women. Vessels, saith God, that would take forth the word, even the sword of the Spirit, who would use it for even the glory and honor of their Lord and their God. Go forth with my word. Let no man hinder you. Look for me to lift you up, saith the Lord.For even I the Lord God send you out not empty handed. But I send you out with the word. I send you out with the word. I send you out with the word, saith the Lord. Hallelujah!

I believe that as you read these pages, you are going to find that if you are in the ministry, you will be set on fire. If you are presently not interested in ministry, a holy fire will be kindled within you. And if you've never thought about ministry up to this time, get ready, because God is about to cause you to think in a new light.

The Third Utterance

The Holy Spirit spoke to me in these four utterances and said, "The doors into other areas are open now, local and foreign." In Revelation 3, the Lord says:

> *I know thy works: behold, I have set before thee an open door; and no man can shut it: for thou hast a little strength, and hast kept My word, and hast not denied My name.*
>
> Revelation 3:8

'Tor yeah, the Spirit of the Lord would say, I open doors. I have opened a door before you; let no ma hinder you. Let no one hinder you. Let not the things of the world hinder you. The door is open before you. You say, Lord I cannot go now. There is no way I can do this thing now. I the Lord your God say, Move now. For I the Lord your God say, Move now. The door is before you. Let not the Lord come and find you've entered not therein. There are those dying in sin, says the Lord. There are those dying in sin and need the word of God. I send you to them that are dying. I send you to them that are suffering. Go in My name and in My might and you shall indeed see wonders, saith the Lord. Let not the enemy put fear in your heart. For I am not the God of fear. I am the Lord your God and I am the God of might, saith the Lord. The devil would love to steal, kill and rob from you of even My blessings that I would desire to pour out upon you, says the Lord. Walk through the door now, says the Lord. Move through the door now, says the Lord. Move in Mine anointing; move in My spirit. And even behold the moving power of almighty God in and around your life, saith the Lord." Hallelujah!

We serve a great and a mighty God, Who is wonderful beyond our hearts' imaginations.

The Fourth Utterance

The evening when the Holy Spirit began to give me all four utterances of this prophetic word, the fourth one took a little to become clear to me because as I lay before *God,* it came gradually, piece by piece. This was because there are actually twelve main statements in this utterance. I urge those with a God-given ministry to pay careful attention.

God said to me in the fourth utterance, "Randy, I show you twelve spirits that are attacking the vessels of honor. And some have difficulty getting out of the grasp of those spirits, and they need to be recognized and as the word says, cast out or cast down." God then gave me these verses from Second Corinthians 10:

> *For though we walk in the flesh, we do not war after the flesh: (For the weapons of our warfare are not carnal, but mighty through God to the pulling down of strong holds;) Casting down imaginations, and every high thing that exalteth itself against the knowledge of God, and bringing into captivity every thought to the obedience of Christ.*
>
> II Corinthians 10:3-5

God then said to me, "'Randy, listen." And over the space of the next thirty to sixty minutes, God spoke to me, giving me these prophecies. He gave them to me one at a time, and I digested them and made notes as best I was able.

He told me that there are twelve spirits hindering the people of God from doing everything that God wants them to do. All twelve may not be tormenting any one individual, but if by chance one is hindering you, get ready for the move of the Spirit of God. We are going to take authority over these spirits, and I'm going to pray and you can read my prayer. I'm going to speak a word of prophetic utterance to you. But first here are the twelve spirits that God showed me.

1. The spirit of fearing man
2. The spirit of fearing failure
3. The spirit of slothfulness
4. The spirit that hinders, always seeming to be in the way right when you're about to work things out.
5. The spirit of confusion
6. The spirit of misdirection. You think you're going in the right way but actually the enemy is taking you in a whole different direction, so you miss the exact spot where God wants you.
7. The spirit of mammon (man or money)
8. The spirit of doubt
9. The spirit of low self-esteem. The feeling that God really wants to use that other person because they are this or that, and God can always do better than me.
10. The spirit of condemnation
11. The spirit of faithlessness
12. The spirit of oppression.

These twelve spirits are tormenting the vessels of God. We need to take authority over them. I'm going to pray. I'm going to speak a prophetic word to you, and I want you to be attentive and listen.

"How many things shall you allow to hold you back? saith the Lord. How many ways have I made clear for you? How many mountains have I moved for you? How many ways have I made clear for you? How many forests have I torn down for you? How many road blocks have I thrown out of your way? How many roads have I made smooth for you? saith the Lord your God. How many things will you allow to keep you back from accomplishing the work I've called you to do? There is a work you must do for Me. There is a work that you must do for Me. Have I not opened up door upon door? Haven't I given you sign upon sign, opportunity upon opportunity, to do my work? Do my work, says the Lord your God. Let not Satan cheat or intimidate you. I've seen your tears. I've heard your cries. I've heard you in the late times of the night, and I've heard you in the early morning hours saying, 'Father God, I cannot complete the work. Even the enemy does come against me, and I can not take any more. Father God, I'm going to fail. Father God, I know not what to do next. Lord, everything is coming against me. I don't know where my strength is. I don't know where my hope.' I, even the Lord your God, am your strength. I, even the Lord your God, am your hope, saith the Lord. You can do nothing without Me. But you can do all things through Me, says the Lord your God. Be not concerned in quantity and size. Be concerned with the quality. Be concerned in the quality of the anointing that I give to you to do My work, says the Lord. Satan desires to hinder you and put you back. I've moved you out, and you go back. I send you forward, and you go back. I give you a mile out ahead, and you go three miles back, says the Lord. It is time to go forward, look not back. Release not the plow; release not the plow. Let not loose of the work of God. But embrace My work that I've given to you tighter than ever, that even the anointing of the Holy Spirit that rests upon you shall bring you into all things, saith the Lord, saith the Lord your God. Satan doth desire to sift you like wheat, but I make intercession for you day and night before the throne of your Father, saith the Lord. And I make intercession for you that you shall be strengthened and you will be strengthened, saith the Lord. Let not him sift you. Be not tormented but be victorious through My Spirit, says the Lord your God. Be victorious by My Spirit, revived and restored, reconciled unto Me, doing all things I called you to do. For in Me there is no error and in Me there is no failing and in Me there is no lacking. So do all things in Me and behold the wondrous works of My hand that shall flow even out of thee, saith the Lord: Hallelujah!

Prayer

Father God, in the name of Jesus I break the powers of hell. I bind every spirit of fear of man and fear of failing. Spirits of slothfulness, spirits that hinder, spirits of confusion, spirits of misdirection, spirits of mammon, spirits of doubt, spirits of low self-esteem, spirits of condemnation, spirits of faithlessness, spirits of oppression -I bind and rebuke them. I release anointing unto the vessels of God, and cause them to be loosed and set free to serve the Lord God Almighty. And I bless them. In Jesus' most holy and precious name I pray. Amen.

My brother and sister, now that you have read that prayer, I believe the Holy Spirit is going to have you read it again. And the Holy Spirit is going to have you read it a third time. And the Holy Spirit is going to have you read it a fourth time. And the Holy Spirit is going to have you read it a fifth time. And the Holy Spirit is going to have you read it a sixth time. And a seventh time for some. There is a completion and a perfection in the number seven; there is a restfulness in the number seven. Some are going to read it an eighth time, which represents the beginning of something new. Get ready, God is about to do something new in you. And I am believing in His Holy Spirit that you are going to yield yourself as a vessel of honor. God Bless you. Amen.

The Messenger's Message

T his is the fourth in the recent series of prophetic words that the Spirit of God has given me. I have found that through this series of words enlightenment, wisdom, understanding, and strength has been brought to parts of the body of Christ-not just locally but all over the United States.

The Lord has moved upon me to put together *God's Bow and Arrow; The Four Waves; The Forerunner;* and now this, *The Messenger's Message.* I believe that as it is read it will be constructive and enlightening. Knowledge and wisdom shall be released from the hand of God into those who have a spirit open to receive the word. This message may be primarily to those in five-fold ministry, and especially to those who stand in the office of prophet or have a strong prophetic word ministry. But let us all be aware of this message, as it lines up with the Word of God as have each of the other messages from the Lord. I believe this word will give insight and knowledge and keep us from falling while in a season in which we truly need to stand.

The Prophet's Jealousy

If you read through First Kings 13, you will find that a tremendous move of God has just taken place, as well as a tremendous disobedience to God. Furthermore, there has been a tremendous yielding of a prophet, not to the hand of the Lord, but to the hand of flesh.

In this passage there are three specific words that God gave to the young man of God upon his visiting the king. The young man came to the king with a word from the Lord instructing him in certain things concerning getting the house of the Lord in order. There were things that were not right and were displeasing to God.

The three points I want to bring out are as follows: In verse 17 it says that God instructed the young man of God to *eat no bread* in the city, to *drink no water* in the city, and to *not leave the same way he had come in*. These were three specific words given to the young man of God from the Lord. I don't believe that these instructions were too difficult for anyone to understand.

In fact, I think these instructions were rather simple and clear. There was nothing confusing about this message from God. We know that the man had heard from God because we read of the signs and wonders that followed his prophetic ministry.

Verse 11 points out the first thought I want to give to you: "Now there dwelt an old prophet in Bethel; and his sons came and told him all the works that the man of God had done that day in Bethel: the words which he had spoken unto the king, them they told also to their father."

Now I know it does not say it, but I see something very clearly in verse 11: If I am the prophet in a city and another prophet comes from outside my city to deliver a word, if my flesh is not under subjection to the Father in heaven, jealousy will raise its ugly head. I see jealousy in this verse. The sons of the old prophet came and told him of the move of God and what had taken place. They told the old prophet everything. This is what I see in verse 11. I think that immediately the question rose up in his heart, Why didn't the Lord show me? I am the prophet in this city. Why didn't the Lord use me? Why wasn't I called when this young man of God came so I could discern the word to make sure it was the truth?

If we are not careful we may also find ourselves questioning the move of God. We must not allow jealousy and carnality to dwell in us and raise up against others whom God has chosen to speak through. We must be very careful to keep ourselves under the blood covering of the Lord Jesus Christ, not giving way to jealousy, which is the first area that I wanted to mention.

The problem of jealously was not only back then, but I believe it is an even greater problem today as we approach the second coming of Christ. We know that there are many attacks of the devil both in the world and in the Church. There are also many men and women of God who still have a problem with their flesh. We need to get our flesh in check so that we don't lead others to destruction. I'm not talking about just leading the sheep in the wrong direction, but I'm also talking about leading other men and women of

God in the wrong direction, and all because we have allowed ourselves to get out of control.

Jealousy is sin. Jealousy is carnal. Human jealousy is ungodly. (There is a godly jealously, however. It is a jealousy on behalf of God's Kingdom. Consider Paul's fatherly jealousy for the purity of the Corinthian church [see II Corinthians 11:1-3].) We must not allow the devil to entice us to be jealous of our brethren-how the Lord is using them and moving in their lives. We ought to rejoice that the Lord is using them rather than becoming envious of them. This will only open the door for Satan to use us. We are vessels of God, and we must not open the door to ungodly jealousy. Let us instead yield ourselves to the hand of the Most High God.

The Prophet's Lie

Part Two has three areas that are quite clear. First Kings 13:18 says, "He said unto him, I am a prophet also as thou art; and an angel spoke unto me by the word of the Lord, saying, Bring him back with thee into thine house, that he may eat bread and drink water. *But he lied unto him:*

Now there are three things going on here: one I believe is pride or boasting. You may ask, Where? My answer is this: the man comes to the prophet and says, "Oh, I am a prophet just like you." I don't believe he needed to make his title known. The calling of God speaks for itself.

The second thing is that lying takes place. He tells the prophet that he has had an angelic visitation, which was an outright lie. He has had no angelic visitation. Verse 18 says this very clearly at the end: "But he lied unto him." The old prophet of God lied to the young man of God. And I believe it was largely because of jealousy.

Now why did the young man of God, though he knew what God had spoken to him, go back with the old prophet of God. I believe out of respect for his elder. Now I know that the Word of God does say we should honor our elders, showing respect for those who are older whether chronologically or spiritually. I understand this. But if they are not in line with the Word of God, and if they are not flowing with the Spirit of God, I do not need to give ear to them when it involves the workings of the Lord. Out of respect we listen to those who have an established ministry. Yet, what they have to say must be in accord with God's word. Revelation 2:11 says, "He that hath an ear, let him hear what *the Spirit* saith unto the churches.

The third thing in verse 19 is that the young prophet went back with the older man and ate bread and drank water in his house. That goes back to verse 17 and the three points that God had specifically told him not to do: Do not eat bread there, do not drink water there, and do not leave the same way you came in. The young man of God suddenly found himself in the grip of disobedience. The Bible says clearly that disobedience is sin, and this young man of God suffered greatly for his sin.

The Prophet's Disobedience

The Bible says, "Obedience is better than sacrifice." Obedience to whom? Obedience to man?

Obedience to God? In all things we must ultimately be obedient to God. But what happens if a man gives me a word from God? If it's a true word from God, I must obey it. But what if a man of God gives me a word that varies from the specific instructions I have received from God? The best thing I can say is this: If a prophet of God, male or female, delivers a word to you that is different from what God has been speaking to you, ill"8t check it out with your Father. God may have made adjustments in your work or in your vision or in the direction of your ministry. If you find that the prophet has missed it, disregard what he says and go forth in the power and anointing of God.

I believe we need to know from whom we are receiving words. For many of our men and women of God, the anointing they walk in speaks for it self. When you have faith in the servant of God, it means that you can also have faith in the word of God that God gives him to deliver to you. In such a case we must be obedient to God's vessel. All I'm saying is what the Scripture has said: *Try the spirits and see if they be of God.*

The young man of God never would have died if he hadn't been disobedient, even though he was being respectful to his elder. The problem was, the old prophet had brought him, not a word of the Lord, but a lie. The young man did not die because of a mistake; he died because of his disobedience. All disobedience is sin. He not only ate and drank in the city, but once he had heard the real word of the Lord, that he was in disobedience and had not done what God said, he ran from the city the same way he had entered. This had been a warning from God: Don't leave the same way you came in. Though the old prophet prophesied truth to the young man of God, he still caused his death.

Let us not only be obedient to the Word of God, but let us also be obedient to the Spirit of God. Let us be obedient to those who move in the anointing of God. And let us also be obedient to God's movement, that we can fulfill the work He has given us to do and show ourselves to be good and faithful servants. The verses that follow show the importance of obedience:

A blessing if you obey the commandments of the Lord your God, which I command you this day: And a curse, if ye will not obey the commandments of the Lord your God, but turn aside out of the way which I command you this day, to go after other gods, which ye have not known.

Deuteronomy 11:27-28

Ye shall walk after the Lord your God, and fear him, and keep his commandments, and obey his voice, and ye shall serve him, and cleave unto him.

Deuteronomy 13:4

Know ye not, that to whom ye yield yourselves servants to obey, his servants ye are to whom ye obey; whether of sin unto death, or of obedience unto righteousness?

Romans6:16

Seeing ye have purified your souls in obeying the truth through the Spirit unto unfeigned love of the brethren, see that ye love one another with a pure heart fervently.

I Peter 1:22

Then Peter and the other apostles answered and said, We ought to obey God rather than men.

Acts 6:29

If ye be willing and obedient, ye shall eat the good of the land.

Isaiah 1:19

Allow me to expound on two of these verses just to press obedience to your spirit-man.

Acts 5:29 says, "Then Peter and the other apostles answered and said, We ought to obey God rather than men. Though every man may be a liar, let God be true. God does not lie. He is not a man that He can lie. We need to be attentive as to how God speaks

46

to us: whether it be through His servants, by His Holy Spirit, by sending us messages through angelic beings, or by speaking to us through His Word. Let us also be attentive to what God is saying. Let us yield ourselves to the Holy Spirit. Let us acknowledge that the Lord is doing something. Unless we are attentive to God, we may find ourselves being attentive to man. Acts 5:29 is very clear-when there is a choice to be made, we must choose to obey God rather than men.

Isaiah 1:19 contains some very strong words. The prophet says, "If ye be willing and obedient, ye shall eat the good of the land. If you are a willing vessel; if you are an obedient vessel; then you will eat the good of the land. You will be increased with the increase of God if you are a willing and an obedient servant. Remember, obedience is *better* than sacrifice.

The Bible says woe be unto you when all men speak well of you. Everyone is not going to be your friend. Everyone is not going to understand you. But be obedient to the voice of God. As we obey God we will see more fruitfulness and more blessing in our lives as pastors, evangelists, teachers, prophets, and apostles. But this is not limited to five-fold ministers. It also applies to singers, praise leaders, intercessors, counselors or any other ministry of the Lord. In whatever area we serve, obedience will bring greater fruitfulness to our lives.

The Death of the Prophets

I believe very strongly that as of today's date, which is May 29, 1991, we have already entered into what the Lord is showing me. You say, what do you mean? I believe that we are going to see (and are already seeing) prophets of God challenging the authority of other prophets from the pulpit. We are going to hear of prophets accusing other prophets openly of being false. We are going to hear of prophets of God preaching lies in order to bring attention to themselves as the old prophet did in First Kings. They will do this so that other prophets will acknowledge who is in their midst.

We need to be attentive, discerning and aware. The Spirit of the Lord is able to guide us into truth so that we will not fight against one another. Our fight is against the devil, not one another. Our job is to destroy the kingdom of hell. Our job is to proclaim the gospel of peace. Our job is to bring the message of salvation.

As I often say at Bread of Life Fellowship, if you have nothing good to say, don't say anything at all.

Let only praises come out of your mouth. Don't be like the old prophet, who found himself unable to deal with someone new coming upon the scene. God is raising up many new vessels. Brothers and sisters, let us recognize that the harvest is truly white and ready to be harvested. The problem is that the laborers are few. *As* far as I am concerned, God can raise up as many as He wants, because no individual can reach this entire world all on his own. Let's acknowledge one another instead of trying to destroy one another.

Even the disciples came and said to Jesus, "Lord, we caught one that was using your name, healing the sick in your name and such. And we forbid him to do so because he is not one of us: And Jesus said to His disciples, "If he is not against us, then he must be for us." Brethren, let us hear the voice of God. Discern and try the hearts of men, and stop operating and moving in the realm of the flesh. Let us cause life to flow into each other. Life and death are in the power of the tongue. The tongue spoke death to a young man of God because the old prophet refused to be content and to give God praise for using someone else.

Let's not speak death to each other, but let's speak life and give praise to God for one another. Let us all be involved in doing the work of the Lord, getting the Church ready for the second coming of Jesus Christ.

God has been showing me clearly through First Kings 13 that the ministry of many of the older prophets is coming to an end. They will soon be going home to meet the Lord. Some of them feel threatened, intimidated and angry at times, jealous because God is raising up many new prophets. Some of the young prophets are jealous of the older ones. I ask that the Church be prayerful, very prayerful.

We may think we have seen shaking in the Body of Christ over the years, but we are about to see shaking like never before. We are about to see the actual death of prophets, both physically and spiritually. The prophets will not die only because of disobedience, but also because there are those who are tormented by spirits of jealousy. This shall also prove to take its toll on many of God's vessels. Harm may come to them because of their disobedience, just like the lion waited for the young man of God to fulfill Gods judgment. We all know that if you bad-mouth someone long enough, it will begin to affect them and the things that happen round about them.

Please let us be careful. Let us not kill our own. Let us not put our own on the altar of sacrifice. Jesus was the perfect sacrifice. Let us not cut each other into pieces. The Bible speaks clearly in Matthew 18 that if anyone has a fault with his brother, he should go to him and confront him over it. Clear the air. Speak well with one another.

A Final Word of Prophesy: "For yeah, saith the Lord, are ye not all My children? Are ye not all My children? saith the Lord. Does not my heart go out to all of you? Does not My Holy Spirit use you? For even some have one gift and some have three, and some may have five or more. But does not My Holy Spirit use all My children? saith the Lord your God. Let not Satan trick you. Allow not the enemy to deceive you, to lie to one another and say it is my Holy Spirit. Allow not your flesh to become jealous or envious of your brothers or sisters who have come through the same blood that you have come through, saith the Lord. But be obedient to My Spirit. Be attentive to My voice. Hearken not to the will of man or to the will of the flesh. But hearken to the voice of God and to the things of the Lord. For even I the Lord your God am a great and a mighty God, and I seek out them that would serve me with a whole heart, saith the Lord. I seek after them that would serve me with all their mind, all their strength, all their soul, all their spirit with every fiber of their being. Let not the enemy cause the prophets to be slain on your altars and in your streets, saith the Lord your God. Love ye one another as I have loved you. Pray for one another even as I now pray for you and allow My Spirit to have its divine way in your life, saith the Lord, that you may be all that I desire you to be even in these times and days. For even Satan is as a roaring lion going about seeking whom he may devour. But even I the Lord your God have put a shielding round about thee, and a shielding of Mine anointing round about thee, and even I the Lord have given My angels charge over thee lest thou dash thy foot against a stone.

"Be aware of the traps of the enemy. Let him not catch you unawares, saith the Lord. For the anointing that I have given unto you is for the purpose of winning souls and shaking the kingdom of hell and building the Kingdom of your God. Do these things and prosper, saith the Lord. Do these things and be encouraged, saith the Lord. And even I say to thee again, Love ye one another, for even I the Lord your God doth love thee, saith the Lord. Amen."

This writing has truly moved and touched me. I pray it does the same to you. And I pray that the Lord Jesus Christ cause the divine purpose of the Father to be done in you. God bless you. Amen.

Printed in the United States
by Baker & Taylor Publisher Services